The Man Who
Ate a Car

D1502476

**Other Young Yearling Books by Stephen Mooser
You Will Enjoy:**

YEARLING BOOKS/YOUNG YEARLINGS/YEARLING CLAS-SICS are designed especially to entertain and enlighten young people. Patricia Reilly Giff, consultant to this series, received her bachelor's degree from Marymount College and a master's degree in history from St. John's University. She holds a Professional Diploma in Reading and a Doctor-ate of Humane Letters from Hofstra University. She was a teacher and reading consultant for many years, and is the author of numerous books for young readers.

For a complete listing of all Yearling titles, write to Dell Readers Service, P.O. Box 1045, South Holland, IL 60473.

THE
CREEPY
CREATURE
CLUB

The Man Who Ate a Car

and Tons of Other Weird True Stories

◆

Stephen Mooser

Illustrated by George Ulrich

A YOUNG YEARLING BOOK

Published by
Dell Publishing
a division of
Bantam Doubleday Dell Publishing Group, Inc.
666 Fifth Avenue
New York, New York 10103

ISBN: 0-440-40460-6

Printed in the United States of America

May 1991

10   9   8   7   6   5   4   3   2   1

CWO

*This book is for
Olga Litowinsky.*

Contents

—————— ◆ ——————

Chapter *1*

———— ♦ ————

The Man Who Ate a Car

The Creepy Creature Clubhouse is filled with lots of weird and scary things. Monster posters cover the walls. A big rubber spider hangs from the ceiling. And scary sounds, moans and groans, are always playing on the tape recorder.

The strangest things, though, aren't hanging on the walls or dangling from the ceiling. They're hidden away in the pages of the Creepy Creature scrapbook. For years the members have been cutting things out of newspapers and magazines. Then they've pasted them into this special

1

book. Some of the stories are scary. Some are funny. And some are just plain weird. All of them, as far as we know, are true.

It's a stormy summer day. All the Creepy Creatures have gathered at the clubhouse. Outside it's thundering and lightning and raining. Inside it's gray and creepy and warm. Just the way the members of the club like it.

"Won't you sit down," says Henry Potter, guiding Ginger Stein over to a long green couch. As usual a wisp of his hair is sticking up in back. Like a feather. "Please, make yourself uncomfortable," he adds, grinning.

"We've got a treat," says Rosa Dorado. Her brown eyes sparkle. "We're going to show you our favorite stories. The ones we've put in the Creepy Creature scrapbook."

Bending down, she sets the heavy scrapbook on the couch. "Who wants to go first?" she asks, looking around the clubhouse. "Who wants to share their favorite weird story?"

"Me! Me! Choose me," says Henry Potter, jumping up and down and waving his arms in Rosa's face. "I don't mean to brag, but I know just where to find the weirdest stories of all."

Everyone laughs. Henry is always bragging.

Rosa sighs. "All right," she says. "You can go first. But please don't hog the whole show. Everyone has a story to tell. Everyone wants to share."

Henry bows his head and pretends to look hurt. "I wouldn't think of hogging the show," he says. "Hey. I'm the greatest sharer in the world." He blows on his knuckles. Then rubs them on his chest. "Maybe the greatest in the universe."

Rosa groans and points at the book. "Just show us your great story," she says. "Everyone is waiting."

Henry winks, bends over, and flips open

the book. "Wait no longer, my creepy friends. Check this out. Here are my favorite stories, the weirdest in the world."

"Yeah," mumbles Rosa. "Just like some people I know."

The Man Who Ate a Car

"In 1970 Leon Sampson, an Australian strongman, won a bet for nearly twenty thousand dollars by eating a car!" said Henry, beginning the story. "It took him four years. But he did it. Little by little he ate the tires, the windshield, even the radio. The whole thing!"

"Yuck," said little Melvin Purdy, interrupting. "How can anyone eat a car?"

"He probably mixed the car up with his regular food," said Henry. "For instance, he might have ground up a bit of windshield and sprinkled it over his eggs at breakfast. Maybe at lunch he mixed a slice of tire in with his hamburger."

4

"I've had hamburgers like that," said Rosa, laughing.

"Wait. There's more to the story," said Henry. "When Bryn Williams, from London, England, heard about Leon, he got mad. Williams, you see, was a famous eater too. 'I can do better than Leon,' he said. Supposedly he went right into training. According to Williams he was going to top Sampson by eating a bus!"

Melvin scrunched up his little nose. "Did he do it, Henry? Did he eat the bus?"

"I haven't heard," said Henry. "Maybe he's still working on it. Perhaps today he's cooking up a special dinner. Something like bus-floor stew."

"I think I had that last week," said Rosa. "In the school cafeteria."

Everyone laughed. Then Henry said, "Here's another short story about food. I think you're going to like it too."

Ouch!

"In Malaysia some people train monkeys to climb trees and pick coconuts. A few years ago a man was walking under a palm tree when suddenly a monkey leapt down and grabbed his head. The monkey must have thought his head was a coconut! He grabbed the man's head and twisted. The monkey's owner came to the man's rescue. The monkey went back to work in the tree. And the man went to the hospital with a sprained neck."

The Man Who Vanished in Plain Sight

"Let me tell you one more story," said Henry. He flipped through the scrapbook. "Ah, here it is. It won't take long to tell."

"I hope not," said Rosa. "Remember. You promised not to hog the show."

"Rosa. Trust me," said Henry. "As soon

7

as I'm done I'll disappear, just like David Lang."

"David Lang?" said Ginger. She scrunched up her freckled nose. "Who was he?"

"The man who disappeared, in plain sight," said Henry. He sighed. "As long as you insist, I guess I'll have to tell you about him."

"Who's insisting?" said Rosa.

"Listen up," said Henry, ignoring Rosa and lowering his voice. "Let me tell you about one of the most famous mysteries in U.S. history. Some people say it never happened. Many others say it did." Henry paused and looked from face to face. "I'll let you decide."

Melvin gulped. "I hope this isn't scary."

Henry grinned. "I'll let you decide."

Then he rubbed his hands together gleefully and began.

"In 1880 David Lang was living on a farm with his wife and two children," said

8

Henry. "The farm was near the small town of Gallatin, Tennessee. One hot summer day the whole family was outside. David told everyone he was going out into his field. His wife and children waved and watched him walk away. It had been a dry summer. The grass was short and brown. The field was flat. No trees or big rocks blocked anyone's view. David had walked about one hundred yards when a buggy came down the road drawn by a horse. Seated in the buggy was David's brother-in-law and his good friend Judge Peck.

"The judge waved to David. David turned and waved. Then, before everyone's eyes, David suddenly disappeared! *Poof!* One minute he was there. The next he wasn't. Just like that. *Poof!*"

"Really? He just vanished?" said little Ollie Morton. His eyes were round as silver dollars. "Then what happened?"

"Well," continued Henry, "at first everyone was too stunned to move. Then Mrs.

Lang screamed. Judge Peck and David's brother-in-law jumped from the buggy. And the children ran out into the field, calling their father."

"And was he there?" asked Rosa. Even she sounded amazed.

"Nope, he had disappeared," said Henry. "At first they thought he had fallen into a hole. Or a crack. But they didn't find any holes. Or cracks. Or anything.

"After a while Mrs. Lang rang a big bell. Neighbors came running. They thought that someone had been hurt. Or that there was a fire. When they got to the farm, Judge Peck and Mrs. Lang told them what had happened. Everyone went right to work with picks and shovels. They dug up the ground. But they didn't find a thing. David Lang had simply vanished. Without a trace."

Henry lowered his voice. He leaned in close to the other Creepy Creatures and continued.

10

"Night came," he said in a bare whisper. "They lit torches. They searched on. Still they couldn't find David Lang."

"They—they couldn't?" said Ollie, his voice shaking.

"Nope," said Henry. "Not that day. Or the next. Or the next one either.

"Time passed. Fall came. Then winter. Word of the mystery spread. People came from all over to investigate. They dug up the ground even more. But under the field they just found solid rock."

"Wow," said Rosa. "That is a weird story."

Henry raised his hand. "Wait. There's more. In the spring things got even weirder."

"Weirder?" said Ollie. He put his hands over his ears, as if he couldn't stand to hear any more. But you could see his hands weren't on very tight. He didn't want to miss anything.

11

"Yep," said Henry. "In the spot where Lang vanished, farm animals would not eat. So the grass grew tall in that spot. Even bugs seemed to stay away from the grassy mystery spot.

"Then one day David's children Sarah, who was eleven, and George, who was eight, were playing near the tall grass. For fun Sarah called, 'Father, Father, are you there?' "

"Don't try to tell us he answered," said Rosa.

"Not at first," said Henry. "But then the two children both yelled it together, 'Father, Father, are you there?'

"They did it four times. Then, suddenly, a voice came floating out of the grass. It said, 'Help! Help me, please!' "

Everyone gasped.

"It was their father's voice," said Henry. "No doubt about it. They could hear him. But, hard as they tried, they couldn't see him."

Henry had everyone's attention now. He licked his lips and went on.

"After a few minutes Sarah and George ran to the house and got their mom. She hurried out into the field. 'David! David!' she cried. 'Where are you? What happened?'

" 'Help me! Help me!' came his reply."

Henry paused to catch his breath. Then continued.

"For the next few days Mrs. Lang and the children called to David. But 'Help me' was the only thing he said. Little by little his voice began to fade. At last he could no longer be heard. Like David himself, the voice had vanished."

Henry smiled and folded his arms across his chest. "And that, my Creepy Creature friends, was the last that anyone ever heard from David Lang. Didn't I tell you it was a good story?"

"Is that story really true?" asked Ginger. She looked quickly around the room, as if maybe David Lang was about to reappear and scare them all silly.

"Some people say it's true, some don't," said Henry. "Some people thought that maybe he was picked up by an invisible flying saucer. Or stepped into another dimension."

"But then how could he still be there months later?" said Rosa. "Wouldn't the flying saucer have flown away?"

"Good point," said Henry. He raised a finger. "Some people think the story started as a rumor. Maybe it was like the game telephone, where the story changes each time it is told. Maybe Mr. Lang just left one night. The next day his wife said, 'David just disappeared. I don't know where he went.' Then other people changed the story every time they told it."

"Yeah, maybe," said Ollie. He was hoping the story wasn't true.

Henry smiled and raised a single eyebrow. "But maybe it was true. And it hap-

14

pened just the way I told it. I've heard there are people in Gallatin today who knew grandparents who were alive when he disappeared. They say it was true. Like I said before, I'll let you decide."

Did You Know?

The cost of raising an average-sized dog from birth to eleven is just over six thousand dollars.

Chapter 2

♦

The Talking Horses

Melvin Purdy reached over the couch. He turned a page in the scrapbook and said, "I have a favorite story too. It's about someone who went into the future. Let me find it for you."

Usually no one paid any attention to Melvin. But this time Rosa did.

"I like that story too," she said. She patted Melvin on the head. "Go on. See if you can find it."

"Whoa. Wait a minute," said Henry. "That story is okay. But I know one even better. It's about some horses—that talked!"

17

Rosa gasped. Then glared at Henry. "I thought you said you weren't going to hog the show. Melvin has a good story. Let him have a turn."

Henry ignored Rosa. He slapped Melvin on the back and whispered into one of his big ears. "Talking horses. You don't run into those every day. What do you say? Let me show the story to Ginger."

"Well . . ." said Melvin.

"You really should wait," whispered Henry. "You know what they always say, save the best for last!"

"Well, my story is pretty special," said Melvin. He rubbed his little chin. "Maybe it would be better if I waited. Still—"

"I knew you'd see things my way," said Henry, cutting him off. "Hand me the scrapbook. You're going to love these stories."

"Stories!" said Rosa. "I thought you were going to tell just one."

18

"The others are super short. And super funny too," said Henry. "Trust me. I'll be done in a second."

Rosa fiddled with a strand of her long black hair and shook her head. "Henry Potter, you're amazing," she said.

"I am pretty amazing," said Henry. "But I know something even more amazing than me."

"More amazing than Henry the hog," said Rosa, laughing. "What possibly could that be?"

"The stories I'm about to tell," said Henry. "Listen up."

Surprise!

"A few years ago a man in Minden, Louisiana, caught a two-pound black bass in a nearby lake," said Henry. "The man took the fish home and put it in his sink. He put his finger in the fish's mouth to start cleaning it when . . . ouch! A small snake bit

19

him. The fish must have eaten the snake just before it was caught!"

Ollie made a face. "Yuck. How could anyone, even a fish, eat a snake?"

"Animals eat all kinds of things," said Henry. "Just ask Lattie's owner."

"Who is Lattie?" asked Ollie.

"The dog in the next story," said Henry. "A dog with a very strange appetite."

Stomachache

"In Wareham, Massachusetts, Lattie, a large Labrador retriever, was taken to the vet," said Henry. "Lattie's owner said she hadn't been eating well. The vet took an X ray. No wonder her stomach was upset. Somehow she had swallowed a ten-inch-long wrench! The vet operated and took out the wrench. Now Lattie is fine. But she is probably not allowed near the tool drawer."

"Lattie ought to meet the man who ate a

car," said Rosa. "They both like the same kind of food."

"Lattie ought to meet the horses in the next story," said Henry. "She could use some of their brains."

The Talking Horses

Henry turned the page. Then cleared his throat. "All right, everybody. This is what you've been waiting for."

"You mean you're finally going to let someone else speak," said Rosa.

"In a way," said Henry, "I am. I'm going to let Clever Hans tell the next story."

"Clever Hans?" said Melvin. "He's not in our club."

"Of course he isn't," said Henry. "He's a horse. A talking one."

"Really?" said Melvin.

"Really," said Henry. "If you want, I'll tell you his story."

"Well . . ." said Melvin.

21

"I knew you'd want to hear the story," said Henry. He turned a page in the scrapbook. Then cleared his throat again, loudly.

"What a hog," mumbled Rosa.

"Nope," said Henry. "What a horse."

Then, after clearing his throat for the final time, he began.

"Clever Hans lived in Germany in the early 1900s," said Henry. "To some people Hans was the 'world's smartest horse.' To others he was the 'world's biggest fake.' "

Henry looked up from the scrapbook.

"Real or fake? No one still knows. But these are the facts:

"Clever Hans was owned by a man named Von Osten. Von Osten had some strange ideas. He was sure he could teach Hans to talk. At first the people in his town of Elberfeld thought he was crazy. But soon they were saying:

" 'Clever Hans can tell time.'

" 'The horse can add.'

22

" 'I saw him read a few words.'

"Soon scientists came from all over. They studied Hans. 'It has to be a fake,' they said. 'Any fool knows horses can't add.' "

"Even I know that," said Ollie. He puffed out his chest. "Horses are good runners, but they're not talkers or readers."

Henry pointed a finger at Ollie. "You're just like the people who lived near Von Osten. They laughed too. (Some said that Von Osten was giving Hans signals without realizing it. A raised eyebrow, for instance, might mean 'Nod yes.') Poor Mr. Von Osten couldn't take it. His heart broke. And within a year he was dead."

Henry shook his head. Then wiped a pretend tear from his eye.

"Luckily, this is not the end of the story," said Henry, smiling. "For, even though his master was dead, Clever Hans lived on. He moved to a farm owned by a man named Karl Krall. Krall was a rich

23

man who believed in Von Osten's ideas. He owned lots of other animals, including two beautiful Arabian horses named Muhammad and Zarif. These two horses soon turned out to be as smart as Clever Hans, maybe even smarter. Within months Krall had trained them to do hard math problems. When people came to Krall's stables, this is what they would see:

"Krall would write a problem on a board. For instance it might be 23 plus 45. Almost at once the horses would 'tap' out the answer with their feet. They would tap out the tens with their left feet. And tap out the ones with their right feet. So, to give the answer to 23 plus 45, they would tap six times with their left feet. Then they would tap eight times with their right. And they would have the correct answer, 68."

"Whoops," said Ginger. She put her hand to her mouth and giggled. "I thought the answer was 65."

"Math wasn't the only thing Krall taught

his horses," said Henry. "He taught them how to read and write too."

"Really?" said Ollie. He scratched his head and wrinkled his face. "How did he do that?"

"It was really very simple," explained Henry. "Krall made up a big alphabet chart and hung it on the wall. The letter *M*, for example, would be in the third square from the left and the second row down. To point out the *M* the horse Zarif would tap three times with his left hoof. Then two times with his right. At first it took a long time to spell a word. But soon the horses were tapping out words so fast that Krall could barely keep up."

"What kind of things did they write?" asked Rosa. "Horse stories?"

"Sort of," said Henry. "In Krall's book, *Thinking Animals,* he wrote that one day Zarif was having trouble tapping.

" 'What's wrong?' asked Krall.

" 'My leg hurts,' tapped Zarif.

"Another time Zarif tapped, 'Albert hit Hans.'

"Krall checked with Albert, his young helper.

" 'Is this true?' he asked.

" 'Yes,' said Albert. 'I guess Zarif saw me.' "

"I bet it was all a trick," said Rosa. "And Krall was only horsing around."

Everyone laughed.

Then Henry said, "Lots of people, including some important scientists, didn't believe Krall either. Some of them thought Krall was giving secret hand signals. To prove them wrong, Krall bought a blind horse named Berto. He trained him a special way. Then he gave him some problems. Berto worked them perfectly. Since he was blind, he couldn't have been watching for signals. And to this day no one has ever fully explained how the horses added and spelled."

Henry smiled. Then folded his arms

across his chest. "Pretty smart horses, huh?"

"Not as smart as our dog, Flip," said Melvin. "He knows the answers to lots of questions too." Melvin looked over at the little gray dog who was the club's mascot. "Tell me, Flip, how does sandpaper feel?"

Flip perked up his ears.

Henry rolled his eyes. "Don't be silly. Flip can't talk. He's not smart like the horses."

"He's smarter," said Melvin. "Just watch. Go on, Flip. Tell Henry how sandpaper feels."

"Ruff!" went Flip.

And everyone laughed. Everyone but Henry.

Did You Know?

On May 6, 1970, Yuichiro Miura of Japan skied down Mount Everest, the highest mountain in the world. At one point he was going more than a hundred miles an hour!

Chapter 3

♦

The Long, Long Fall

Rosa picked up the big scrapbook and moved it from Henry's lap to Melvin's lap.

"Now, at last, it's Melvin's turn," she said. "Go ahead. Find the story about the man who went into the future." She gave Henry a dirty look. "And this time let's hope no one interrupts."

Henry held out his hands. "Don't look at me. I'm not going to interrupt. I'd like to go into the future myself. I'm excited to hear how the man did it."

"He flew into the future," said Melvin as

he was thumbing through the book. "He flew there in a plane."

"A plane!" said Henry. He hit his forehead with his hand. "That reminds me of a great story. About a man who fell out of a plane." He looked quickly at the other Creepy Creatures. "Let me read it to you. It's absolutely incredible."

"It's Melvin's turn," said Rosa. "Besides, I'm sure Melvin's story is just as amazing as yours."

"I bet it's even more amazing," said Melvin.

Henry tapped Melvin on the nose. "You got a bet." Then, before Melvin knew what had happened, Henry had taken back the scrapbook. "I'll read my story first. Then you can read yours. Afterward everyone will vote for the one they think is most amazing. Whoever gets the most votes wins the bet!"

"Bet?" said Melvin. He scratched his head.

Henry tapped Melvin again on the nose. "I'm going to win this bet, easy. Just listen to this."

And once again, somehow, the Creepy Creatures found themselves listening to one of Henry's stories.

"In 1942 Germany attacked Russia," said Henry, talking out of the side of his mouth. He was trying to sound like a TV newsman. "Fighting raged on land, on sea, and in the air. One day in January, Lieutenant I. M. Chisov, a Russian pilot, took off aboard his fighter and headed into battle. He had climbed to nearly 26,000 feet when suddenly he ran into some German planes high above southern Russia.

"Pa-*ting!* Pa-*ting!*" said Henry, making the sounds of bullets flying.

"The Germans kept firing. Chisov tried to get away, but he couldn't outrun those bullets. Then, suddenly, *KABOOM!* His plane was hit! And slowly it started to go down.

33

"Chisov fought to save his plane, but he couldn't. The controls had been wrecked. Worse yet, a fire had started in the back. And smoke, black smoke, was beginning to fill the cabin."

"Jump!" said Ollie suddenly. "Put on your parachute!"

"And that's just what Lieutenant Chisov decided to do," said Henry. "He got up and reached for his parachute. Only . . ."

The Creepy Creatures were on the edge of their seats.

"Only what?" they said.

"Only, his parachute was on fire," said Henry. "Now he had two choices. He could either go down with the plane. Or he could jump."

"Jump? From 26,000 feet?" said Rosa. "That's nearly as high as twenty Empire State Buildings stacked end to end."

Henry nodded. "But jump is exactly what Chisov did. He threw himself out of the plane and into the freezing cold air.

34

Mercifully, the fear and the cold made him pass out almost at once. Then down he tumbled toward a forest of tall pines rising up out of a deep blanket of snow.

"Down, down he came at an incredible speed. The first thing he hit was the top of a tall pine. *Whap!* he snapped off a big limb like it was a toothpick. *Whap! Whap! Whap!* he broke off more branches as he hurtled toward the ground. Then . . ."

Henry paused. The Creepy Creatures were waiting, eyes wide, mouths open, for the end of the story.

"Then—KER-*THUD!* Chisov's limp body plowed into the deep snow and lay still. For a moment all was quiet. Then Chisov opened his eyes and looked up through the tree that had helped break his fall. He blinked once. Then twice. Then whispered to himself in amazement, 'I'm alive!'

"Not only was he alive. But he was in pretty good shape besides. He had a few broken ribs, and some bruises. But otherwise he was all in one piece. But then, unfortunately . . ."

"Unfortunately what?" asked Ginger.

"Unfortunately he was soon captured by the German invaders," said Henry. "At first they didn't believe his story. They had seen the plane crash, but they hadn't seen any parachutes.

"But then, just before they took him away, Chisov pointed up at the tree. When the Germans saw the broken branches they realized he was telling the truth, as amazing as it was."

"What happened then?" asked Ginger.

"Chisov was a prisoner until the war was over," explained Henry. "When he got back home he discovered he was famous. Everyone had heard about his fall. He was a national hero."

"He was more than a hero," said Rosa. "He was something else too."

"What?" said Henry.

"Lucky," said Rosa. "Real, real lucky."

While everyone was thinking about Chisov and his lucky landing, Henry began another story. By the time anyone realized what was going on, Henry was well into his next amazing tale. This one he called:

A Strange Rescuer

"One summer night, in the late 1970s, a lady named Candelaria Villanueva was sailing on a small boat near the Philippines," said Henry. "She was about six hundred miles from land when disaster struck—her ship caught on fire."

"Wow, just like Chisov's plane," said Melvin. "Are you going to tell us she didn't have a life jacket, just like Chisov didn't have a parachute?"

"She did have a life jacket," said Henry. "But that was all. Into the warm water she went, six hundred miles from land.

"It was nighttime, dark and scary. In the morning, when the sun finally rose, Ms. Villanueva found herself all alone."

38

"And six hundred miles from land," said Rosa.

"And without a boat," said Ginger. "That lady was in trouble."

"And she knew it," said Henry, continuing. "All day long she floated on the sea. She hoped a ship would pass by soon. She knew she couldn't last long. Then, just as it was again starting to get dark, she felt something bang into her legs."

"Yikes! A shark," said Ollie.

"Nope," said Henry. "It was a giant turtle. It lifted her up on its shell. It had come to her rescue!

"The turtle stayed with her through the night. At one point a little turtle crawled onto her back. 'Every time I got sleepy the little turtle bit me,' said Ms. Villanueva later. 'Maybe he was trying to keep me awake. He didn't want me to fall asleep. For if I did, I might have fallen off the big turtle and drowned.' "

"Ah," said Rosa. She put her hands under her chin. "What neat turtles."

Henry smiled. He wished Rosa thought that he was neat too. He liked her, a lot. Unfortunately, she didn't always like him, especially when he was hogging the book. Sighing, Henry finished the story.

"Late the next day a freighter showed up and spotted Ms. Villanueva," he said. "They lowered a rope and hauled her on board.

" 'After we got her out of the water the turtles circled the ship twice before swimming away,' said one of the men on the boat. 'It was like the turtle wanted to make sure she was safe. No one could believe it.' "

Did You Know?

There is a life-jacket salesman in England named Will Drown.

Chapter 4

◆

Treasure!

"All right, Henry," said Rosa. "You got to tell your stories. Now let Melvin tell us his."

Melvin grinned. He began flipping through the Creepy Creature scrapbook. "It's in here somewhere," he said. "It's the most amazing story of all. About a man who went into the future."

Henry watched Melvin go through the book. He sighed and tapped his foot loudly. Finally, he yawned and said, "By the time you find the story, the future will be here. What's taking so long?"

"It's a big scrapbook," said Melvin. "But it's worth looking for. It's a real treasure."

"Treasure!" said Rosa. "That reminds me of my favorite story in the scrapbook. Anyone want to hear about the biggest treasure of all?"

"Rosa Dorado!" said Henry. "It's Melvin's turn." He shook a finger at his friend. "Now who is trying to hog the show?"

"I'm not trying to hog anything," said Rosa. "I'm trying to help. If you don't want to hear about the Oak Island treasure, that's fine with me. Go ahead, Melvin. I don't care if we don't become billionaires."

"Billionaires!" gasped the Creepy Creatures.

"If we can solve the mystery, that's how much we'll make," said Rosa. "I'm serious. It's the greatest treasure in the world."

Melvin Purdy whistled. "A billion dollars. Wow." He rubbed his hands together and shook his head at the wonder of it. "Whew. That's a lot of money."

"It's a ton," said Rosa. "Want to hear where we can find it?"

"You bet!" said Melvin. He seemed to have forgotten all about the man who went into the future. "Tell us about the treasure. My story can wait. Come on. We got to get that billion dollars."

"But—but," sputtered Henry, "it's not fair. If I had done this you would have called me a hog."

Rosa smiled. "That's right," she said. Then, humming, she flipped to a new page in the scrapbook. "Ah, here it is. The Oak Island treasure. Our ticket to a billion dollars."

The Oak Island Treasure

"Daniel McGinnis was a farm boy who liked to go exploring," said Rosa, reading from the scrapbook. "One day, in 1795, he

43

took a trip to Oak Island, which is in Canada, near Maine. As he was walking around he came to a strange clearing in the woods. In the middle of the clearing the earth had sunk, as if something had been buried there. Treasure, maybe. It was possible, because many years earlier pirates had been seen on that very island."

"Pa-pa-pirates!" said Melvin. "Are they still guarding that treasure? If so, I don't want to go look for it. No way!"

Rosa shook her head. "There haven't been pirates for a hundred years," she said. She leaned in close to Melvin and lowered her voice. "Maybe the pirates' ghosts are still there, though."

Melvin gulped and put a hand to his mouth.

Rosa smiled. "But you shouldn't be afraid. Ghosts aren't real. You know that."

Melvin nodded. But by the way he was rubbing his hands together, it didn't look like he believed her.

"Well," said Rosa, continuing, "the next day Daniel came back to the clearing with two friends. They started digging. Right away they found something. Two feet under the ground were some flat stones. They had been placed together carefully, like tiles.

"Excited, they dug deeper. Twelve feet down they hit something else, a floor of oak logs.

"*We're getting close,* they thought. And so they dug deeper.

"Twenty feet down they hit another floor of oak logs. After days of digging, the hole was twenty-seven feet deep. Still no treasure. Exhausted, they gave up."

"They gave up?" said Henry. "That's it? That's the end of the story?"

"Of course it's not the end," said Rosa. "Nine years later they came back. This time they had more help and money. By now everyone around was sure a big treasure was buried on Oak Island.

45

"Down they dug again. Every ten feet they hit a floor of oak logs. At sixty feet they found parts of some coconuts. At eighty feet they found a large stone. It was covered with strange markings. Now they were sure they were close by. Someone had gone to a lot of trouble to hide something on Oak Island. Whatever it was must have been very valuable."

"Maybe they were hiding oak logs and stones," said Henry, laughing. "And the dumb kids didn't realize it."

Rosa ignored Henry and went on with her story.

"At ninety feet water began seeping into the hole. They pounded a long iron rod into the bottom of the hole. It hit something solid. *The treasure chest!* they thought.

"Night was falling. They stopped work. All that night they talked about what they would do with the money. But in the morning they made a terrible discovery. Overnight the hole had filled with water."

"Couldn't they scoop out the water?" asked Melvin.

"Nope," said Rosa. "No matter how hard they tried, they couldn't pump it out fast enough. More kept flooding in. Finally, they had to give up."

"That's it?" said Henry. "They gave up? That's the end of your story?"

Rosa glared at Henry. "No. That isn't the end of the story."

Henry gulped. He didn't want Rosa to be mad at him. "Please," he said, "go on. You tell the best stories."

Rosa rolled her eyes. Then continued.

"In 1840 some people tried again," she said. "This time they dug a hole alongside the first one. When they got down to ninety-eight feet, they dug across. But they didn't do it right. And everything caved in.

"As the years went by, more and more people tried to solve the mystery of Oak

Island. They discovered that tunnels had been built under the island. The tunnels connected the 'money pit' to the Atlantic Ocean. That's why the hole had flooded."

"Wow," said Melvin. "Whoever hid that treasure did a good job. Whatever they hid must have been worth a lot."

"That's what a lot of people thought," said Rosa. "In fact, in 1909 Franklin Roosevelt, who would be President of the U.S. someday, went to Oak Island and searched. But he didn't find anything either.

"Over the next forty years people tried everything. Bulldozers, high-powered water pumps, metal detectors, dynamite, everything. Still they couldn't get to the treasure.

"Then, in 1971, a TV camera was lowered two hundred and thirty feet into the money pit. Through the muddy water they saw an amazing sight, a treasure chest and the skeleton of a hand!"

Melvin put his hands on his cheeks. "Yikes! A skeleton! Rosa, you lied. You said there weren't any ghosts there."

"Melvin, there's a big difference between a ghost and a skeleton," said Rosa. "Everyone in the Creepy Creature Club should know that."

"There's no difference to me," said Melvin. "They're both the same."

"The same?" said Henry. "How?"

"They're both scary," said Melvin.

Rosa sighed. "Can I finish my story now?"

"Please do," said Henry. "Get to the billion-dollar part."

"That's just what the treasure hunters wanted to do too," said Rosa. "That very day they tried to get the chest. But they were in such a hurry that all they did was stir up the mud. The chest and the hand were never seen again. Both had moved. Probably they had slipped into one of the tunnels that connected to the ocean."

"So they still haven't found the treasure?" said Henry. "It's still under the island somewhere?"

"Yep!" said Rosa, closing the book. "The mystery still hasn't been solved. And the treasure is still waiting."

"What kind of treasure is it?" asked Melvin. He rubbed his hands together and grinned. "Is it bags of diamonds? Rubies? A ton of gold?"

"No one knows for sure," said Rosa. "Lots of people think that the money pit was a pirate bank. Many pirates worked together to build the pit. Then all of them hid their treasure there.

"Others think that the money pit holds the crown jewels of France. They have been missing for hundreds of years. And they'd be worth a billion dollars, at least."

Melvin whistled. "Boy, could I ever use that money."

"Lots of people think the treasure is Inca Indian gold," said Rosa. "The Incas brought it all the way from South America. They were trying to hide it from the Spanish. The Incas were good builders. They would have known how to design the money pit."

"We've got to go after that money," said Melvin. "All we have to do is find out where Oak Island is."

"We also have to get there," said Henry. "Remember, we don't have any cars, just bikes."

"It probably is a long way from here," said Rosa. "Still, that is a lot of money. Someday, somebody is going to find it."

Melvin licked his lips. "And that somebody is going to be me," he said. He rubbed his hands together and looked over at the clock. It was still early in the afternoon. "Maybe we can even go today!"

Rosa laughed. But not Melvin. He was serious. And while Rosa was telling a last short story, Melvin got up and went to the back of the room to find a map.

"Won't my mom be surprised?" he said, rubbing his hands together. "Won't she be amazed when I come home tonight with a billion dollars in my pocket!"

Did You Know?

The loudest noise in recorded history was the explosion on August 27, 1883, of the Krakatoa volcano in the Dutch East Indies. The force of the explosion created a wind that circled the earth seven times. A tidal wave traveled around Cape Horn and lapped at the shore of England, 11,500 miles away. And the noise was heard loud and clear in Texas, 9,000 miles away!

Chapter 5

♦

Inside a Flying Saucer

"**A**ll right, Melvin," said the Creepy Creatures. "It's your turn. Tell us the story about the man who flew into the future."

"Huh?" said Melvin, glancing up from the bookcase in the back of the clubhouse. He looked as if he were a thousand miles away. As it turned out, he was.

"Does anyone have a map of Canada?" he asked. "I want to see how close Oak Island is to River City."

"But what about your story?" asked Rosa. "Don't you want to tell everyone about the man who flew into the future?"

"In a minute. In a minute," said Melvin. He pawed his way through some books. Desperately, he looked for a clue to that billion dollars.

Rosa shook her head. She looked around the room. "Anyone else want to share a weird story?" she asked.

"Ta-ta!" said Henry, raising both hands. "I do!"

Rosa rolled her eyes. "Give someone else a turn." Rosa looked around the room again. "Come on. Who wants to share?"

No one raised a hand.

Henry smoothed down his feather of hair. Then he waved his hand in Rosa's face. "Yoo-hoo," he said. "I got some great stories to tell. One is about a flying saucer and another one is about a fish with a big mouth."

Rosa sighed. Then shook her head. "All right. Tell your stories. No one else could tell a story about a big mouth better than you."

Henry smiled. He thought Rosa had given him a compliment. "Thanks," he said. "Gee. What a nice thing to say."

And at that he opened his big mouth and began.

Lost and Found

"In 1980 a man in Newport News, Virginia, was walking near a canal in a storm," said Henry. "Accidentally he banged his hand and his wedding ring fell off. *Kerplunk!* It dropped into a canal. Two years later a restaurant in a nearby town found the ring. It was inside a fish they had bought! The man's name had been written on the ring. What a surprise he had when he was told the ring had been found!"

"What a double surprise when they told him where it had been," said Rosa, laughing.

"Speaking of being inside things, here's another inside story," said Henry.

Inside a Flying Saucer

"On October 11, 1973, Calvin Parker, who was 19, and Charlie Hickson, 42, went fishing on the banks of the Singing River in Pascagoula, Mississippi," said Henry, beginning his new story. "But the big story that night wasn't the fish they caught. It was the flying saucer that caught them!"

"What did the saucer use to catch them with?" asked Ginger. "Giant alien worms?"

"Giant worms!" gasped Melvin, looking up from the bookcase. "Where are they?"

"In your imagination," said Henry. "Please. This is a serious story." He cleared his throat and continued.

"Both Parker and Hickson worked at a local shipyard," he said. "After getting off work they grabbed their poles and hurried to the river. As a full moon rose overhead, they sat by an old pier, talking and fishing. Finally, around nine, they decided to go home. It had been a good night. And they had caught quite a few catfish."

Henry lowered his voice and tried to sound scary.

"Just as they were packing up, they heard a noise. They turned around and gasped.

"There, just behind them, was a flying saucer!"

Melvin looked up again from the bookcase. When he heard the words *flying saucer* he gasped too.

" 'It was about ten feet long. Kind of egg shaped,' said one of the men, Charlie.

" 'There were flashing blue lights on the front,' said Calvin, his friend."

Henry rubbed his hands together and raised his eyebrows. More than anything, he wanted to show off for Rosa by telling a scary story.

"After a few moments a door opened. Out came three creatures.

" 'They looked like robots. Their skin was like wrinkled metal,' said Charlie. 'They were about five feet tall with stubs

for feet and claws for hands. Neither had a neck. Both had only slits for eyes. And antennas where their ears should have been.'

"Charlie and Calvin were too stunned to move. They stood and watched as the creatures came their way. Calvin said later that they didn't walk. 'They floated,' he said."

"Sounds like they might have been parade balloons," said Rosa. "Was there a parade nearby?"

"Of course not," said Henry. "It was nighttime. Anyway, a balloon couldn't do what the creatures did next."

"Wha-wha-what was that?" asked Melvin. He was paying attention now. It also looked as if he was the only one who was being scared by Henry's story.

"The creatures took hold of Calvin and Charlie and picked them up," said Henry. "Then they carried them to their flying saucer.

"Of course, Calvin didn't remember go-

61

ing to the ship. That's because he fainted the second the aliens touched him."

"I'd faint too," said Melvin.

" 'They took us inside,' said Charlie. 'Next thing I knew, we were floating in this room. A big eye, about the size of a football, floated around us. I think it was taking X rays or something.'

"Finally, after about twenty minutes, the creatures let them go," said Henry.

" 'They carried us back to the river,' reported Charlie. 'Then they got back in their ship and blasted off.' "

"This all sounds like another one of your fishy stories," said Rosa. She yawned. "I thought it was supposed to be scary."

Henry bit his lip. Rosa didn't seem too impressed by his story. "Just wait," said Henry. "It gets even scarier."

"Really?" said Melvin.

"Listen up," said Henry. He lowered his voice again. "Before long Calvin and Charlie decided to report to the sheriff what

62

had happened, even though they didn't think he would believe their story.

"The sheriff's name was Fred Diamond," said Henry. "At first he thought Calvin and Charlie were drunk. So he gave them a test. But the test showed they had not been drinking.

"Next the sheriff made some calls. Two toll bridges went over the river near where the saucer had landed. The men who worked in the tollbooths said they hadn't seen anything.

"The sheriff couldn't figure out what was going on. He thought for sure the men had been lying. He decided to trick them. He put them in a jail cell and hid a tape recorder nearby. He was sure Calvin and Charlie would whisper how they had made up the story. But they didn't. Instead, this is what the sheriff heard:

" 'I've never seen nothing like that in my life before,' said Charlie. 'They better start believing.'

" 'I got to see a doctor,' said Calvin.

" 'They won't believe it, but they better,' said Charlie. 'I knew all along there were people from other worlds up there. I knew all along. But I never thought it would happen to me.'

"And through it all Calvin just kept moaning. 'It's awful. Oh, it's awful.' "

Henry tapped the scrapbook. "Later the sheriff gave them lie detector tests. They both passed. The detector said they were telling the truth." Henry looked at Rosa and wiggled his eyebrows. "Scared yet?"

Rosa put a hand to her mouth and yawned.

But Melvin said, "Wh-what happened next?"

"Well," said Henry, "before long word got out that a saucer had landed in Mississippi, and for a few weeks Calvin and Charlie were famous. Stories about them were in the newspapers. And on TV. People came from all over to ask them questions.

64

"Some people said that Charlie and Calvin really had been on a flying saucer. Others weren't so sure. 'Why hadn't anyone else seen anything?' they asked."

"Yeah," said Rosa.

"But what about the lie detector test?" said Melvin.

"The man who gave them the lie detector test said he was certain that Calvin and Charlie believed they were on a flying saucer," said Henry. He sighed. "However, he also said that it didn't actually mean they were on a UFO. It only meant they believed they were."

"You see," said Rosa. "It probably never happened."

"Well, I think it did," said Henry. "And I know some other people who believed it too."

"Oh, yeah, who? Those far-out fishermen, Calvin and Charlie?" said Rosa.

"Nope," said Henry. "Someone even farther out than them. The aliens!"

Did You Know?

Only humans and one other creature can get a sunburn. The other animal is a pig.

Chapter *6*

❖

The Whale and the Kangaroo

"Melvin, have you found that map of Canada yet?" asked Rosa. "Henry is done. Come on. I can hardly wait to hear your story. The one about the man who went into the future."

Melvin was still busy in the back of the room. Bent over, he was searching through some books.

"Melvin. Come on," said Rosa.

"I'll be there in a minute," said Melvin. He didn't look up. "I can't be a billionaire till I find out where Oak Island is."

Henry rolled his eyes. "He's going to take forever."

"No, he isn't," said Rosa. "In the meantime I'll see if I can find the story."

Rosa quickly began thumbing through the scrapbook. Halfway through, little Ollie Morton suddenly put his hand onto a page.

"Oh, look!" said Ollie. "There's my favorite story. The one about the bad fog."

Henry glared at Ollie. "Wait your turn."

"But it's such a funny story," said Ollie. He put his hand to his mouth and giggled just thinking about it. "Please?"

"Well," said Rosa, "you haven't had a turn."

"That's right," said Henry quickly, trying to impress Rosa. "It's important that we all share the book."

"My story isn't very long," said Ollie.

Rosa glanced over at Melvin. He was looking at a map of Africa. "Melvin is about ten thousand miles off," she said.

"He's never going to find Canada. Not in Africa." Rosa shook her head. "Go on, Ollie. It looks like we do have a few free minutes."

The Head-on Wreck

"One day in 1974 a heavy fog hit Brescia, Italy," said Ollie. "Driving was dangerous. You could see only a few feet ahead. Most people stayed home. Some people that did drive had to stick their heads out of the window to see. Two of these people met on a bridge. They never saw each other till *bang!* They bumped heads. What a surprise! Both drivers went to the hospital. Luckily, neither was badly hurt."

The Creepy Creatures laughed. Ollie grinned. Everyone liked his story. He was so excited, he quickly told them another, this one even funnier than the last.

Hopping Mad

"One afternoon in late 1986 Emilio Tarra was driving outside of Perth, Australia, when he hit a kangaroo," said Ollie. He put a hand to his mouth and giggled, thinking about what was coming next. "When he got out of the car the kangaroo was lying by the side of the road. Mr. Tarra thought it was dead. For a joke he leaned the kangaroo against his car. Then he put his jacket on the kangaroo and got out his camera. For some reason Emilio thought a dead kangaroo wearing his jacket would make a funny picture. But the kangaroo wasn't dead! All at once he woke up. With a mighty swat of his tail he knocked Emilio down. Then he calmly hopped off into the desert wearing Emilio's jacket. In the pocket of his jacket was all Mr. Tarra's credit cards and two thousand dollars in cash."

Rosa laughed. "Did he ever get his money back?" she asked.

"Nope," said Ollie. "That kangaroo left Mr. Tarra broke and hopping mad."

Rosa smiled. "I liked that story."

"Can I tell one more?" asked Ollie. "I promise it's my last." He smiled. "I don't want to be a hog like some people."

Everyone looked at Henry.

"Hey, what did I say?" said Henry.

"Nothing," said Rosa. "And just keep it that way too. Go ahead, Ollie. Tell us another story."

Just like Jonah

"In February of 1891 a whaling boat, *Star of the East,* was off the coast of Argentina," said Ollie.

" 'Thar she blows!' cried a sailor, spotting a large whale.

"The *Star of the East* turned about. The crew hurried onto the deck. A small boat was lowered. The men in the boat paddled after the huge whale. When they got

72

nearby they threw a harpoon into it. The whale lashed out with its tail. *Wham!* The little boat was flipped up into the air. Everyone was knocked into the ocean.

"Quickly the *Star of the East* came alongside," said Ollie. "They put another harpoon into the whale. Others rescued the sailors from the water. Eventually everyone was saved but one. The missing sailor was named James Bartley. The crew figured he had drowned."

"Poor guy," said Ginger.

"Before long the crew had dragged the whale on board," said Ollie, continuing.

"Poor whale," said Rosa.

"You're right, poor whale," said Ollie. "The big guy was dead. Once he was on the ship they started to clean him. They were about to quit for the day when someone noticed something moving in the whale's stomach. When they opened the stomach there was James Bartley. He was doubled up, and passed out. But he was alive!"

"Wow!" said Ginger. "Just like Jonah."

"Just like Jonah is right," said Ollie. "After Bartley had awakened he told everyone what had happened.

" 'I remember being in the water,' he said. 'Then I remember sliding down a dark passage. Finally I blacked out.' "

"Hard to believe," said Rosa.

"Perhaps," said Ollie. "But like all the stories in this book, it's true." He giggled. "Really!"

Did You Know?

It's impossible to sneeze with your eyes open.

Chapter 7

◆

The Man Who Went into the Future, at Last

Melvin finally found the right map. When he saw where Canada was, he almost cried.

"Look how far away it is," he said. "That billion dollars might as well be on the moon."

Rosa smiled. She patted Melvin on the shoulder. "When you get older, you can look for it," she said. "In the meantime why don't you tell us your favorite weird story? The one about the man who flew into the future."

Melvin turned to Henry. "Is it okay with you, Henry? Okay that I tell my story?"

"Don't look at me," said Henry. "Why would I try to stop you? If you want to tell your story, go ahead."

"Are you sure?" asked Melvin.

Henry laughed. "Do whatever you want. If you have a story to tell, go ahead. I'm not the kind of person to butt in."

Now everyone else laughed. And Melvin, at last, could tell his favorite story.

"Victor Goddard was a pilot in the British air force," said Melvin. "One Saturday, in 1935, he flew off for a visit to Scotland. He wanted to see an old family friend, Mrs. Peploe.

"When his plane landed at the airport in Scotland, Mrs. Peploe was waiting.

" 'I was afraid you wouldn't come,' she said. 'A storm is due on Monday. You might not be able to fly home.'

" 'A little rain doesn't scare me,' said

76

Goddard. 'Remember, I've been flying for years. I can handle anything.'

"The next day Goddard asked to go to Drem Airfield," said Melvin, reading from the story in the scrapbook. "Mr. Goddard had used it years before during World War One. He remembered it was not far from Mrs. Peploe's house. Maybe, he thought, he could land there on his next visit.

"The airfield turned out to be in horrible shape. It hadn't been used in years. The roofs on the hangars were falling in. The landing strip was full of holes. To make matters worse, the field had been rented to a farmer. His cows grazed everywhere.

" 'There's not enough room for a bird to land,' he said, laughing. 'I don't think I'll be using this for a while.' "

"When does he go into the future?" asked Henry, interrupting. "That's the part I want to hear."

"Soon," said Melvin. "Just listen. The story is about to get real exciting."

Then Melvin continued.

"On Monday Mrs. Peploe drove Goddard back to his plane," said Melvin. He lowered his voice and tried to sound scary. The way Henry had earlier. "The weather had turned nasty, just like it is today," he said. "Bursts of lightning mixed with thunder ripped the sky. Thick clouds hung over the hills like black drapes. Goddard's plane had an open cockpit. If it rained he'd get soaking wet.

" 'I thought I could get above the clouds,' he said later. 'And so I took off.' "

"Is this it?" asked Henry. He poked his head in front of Melvin's face. "Is this where he goes into the future?"

"Shhh!" said Rosa.

"Poor Goddard couldn't climb out of the storm," said Melvin, ignoring Henry. "Then, at eight thousand feet, his motor suddenly stalled!" Melvin gasped. He seemed surprised even though he was the one telling the story. "Goddard went into a spin. Down he went, out of control. Rain-soaked clouds pressed in like damp cotton. Everything was gray. He didn't know if he was right side up or upside down. All he knew was that he was heading down."

Everybody leaned forward to listen. Melvin grew so excited, he started talking faster and faster.

"At three thousand feet he ran into a pouring rain," said Melvin. "But being wet was not his worry now. In another minute he'd slam into the ground!

"Two thousand feet and still spinning.

"Now one thousand feet.

"Goddard's heart pounded. He was going to die, he knew it. At two hundred feet the clouds thinned out. He could see something! It was a little bay. There was a road and a girl with a baby carriage alongside the bay."

Melvin stood up. He clenched his fists and yelled, "A second to live!

"Goddard yanked at the controls. The plane shuddered. The nose came up just inches from the water. He gave it all the gas he could. The engine screamed and he roared out over the road. The girl with the carriage ducked under Goddard's wing.

"He had made it!"

"Hooray!" went the Creepy Creatures.

"But he wasn't out of trouble yet!" said Melvin.

"Boo!" said the Creepy Creatures.

"Goddard didn't want to climb back into the clouds," said Melvin, continuing. "But he couldn't stay low to the ground either. There were hills somewhere. He knew he needed to find a landmark. He thought he might be near old Drem Airfield. If he could find it he'd know which way to fly. At a hundred fifty miles an hour he whistled above the road. Suddenly, through the gloom, he saw the hangars at Drem!"

Melvin paused and caught his breath. Then he picked up the scrapbook again and said, "What happened next is so amazing, I'll let Goddard's words tell the story.

" 'When I reached the field everything was suddenly bathed in sunlight,' said Goddard. 'The rain had stopped. All the hangar doors were open. Lined out in spick-and-span order were four airplanes. Three of them were biplanes. The fourth was a single-winged plane. I'd never seen anything like it. Another thing that puzzled me was the color of the planes. All of them were yellow. But at the time all air force planes were supposed to be silver.

" 'Some men were pushing a plane out of a hangar. I noticed they were wearing blue overalls. This didn't make sense to me. At the time air force overalls were brown, not blue. I was also surprised that no one looked up at me. I was quite low to the ground. And making a lot of noise. Yet no one looked up. It was as if I wasn't there.'

"Goddard didn't believe his own eyes,"

said Melvin. "He never thought for a moment about landing. A few seconds later he had passed over the field. The clouds and the rain pressed in again. He lifted the nose of the plane skyward. And started to climb.

"This time he made it through the clouds. At seventeen thousand feet he broke into the clear. Within a few hours he was safely back at his base in England.

"At lunch that day he told his story to his friends. They didn't believe him for a second. 'You're crazy,' they said. 'You were seeing things.'

"But Goddard couldn't stop thinking about his amazing flight," said Melvin. "What had happened? Where had he been? What had he seen?"

"The future?" said Henry. "Had he seen the future?"

"Yep!" said Melvin, grinning. "But he didn't realize it till five years later. By then

83

World War Two had started. England began fixing up its old airfields. One of the first to be repaired was Drem. The old hangars were pulled down. New ones were put up. The strip was patched. And planes again roared off its runways. The things Goddard had 'seen' in his vision came true. The air force switched from brown overalls to blue. They began painting their planes yellow instead of silver. Starting in 1939 Drem was filled with yellow 504N biplanes as well as the brand-new Magister single-wing planes."

"I've never heard of anyone else ever going into the future," said Ginger. "Are you sure he wasn't just dreaming? Or maybe he just made some lucky guesses."

"Maybe," said Melvin. "But Goddard doesn't have any doubts—he knows exactly what he saw. He saw the future."

"Wow! Those are amazing stories," said Rosa.

"I told you," said Melvin, grinning.

"Henry was right. The best was saved for last."

"Not so fast," said Henry. "Don't you think my stories were just a little teeny tiny bit better?"

Rosa sighed and shook her head. Henry was such a bragger. "Weird," she said.

"Yeah. You're right," said Henry. "Mine were the weirdest."

"I didn't mean your stories were weird," said Rosa. "What I meant was that you were the weirdest."

Henry beamed. "Really?" Wow! Rosa really did think he was special!

"No doubt about it," said Rosa. "You're the weirdest guy in the world."

"Wonderful!" said Henry. He blew on his knuckles. Then rubbed them on his chest. He didn't care what he was as long as he was the best at it.

Did You Know?

In 1931 Joe Sprinz, a catcher for the San Francisco Seals, caught a baseball dropped eight hundred feet from a blimp. He held on to the ball. But the force sent a mighty shudder through his body. So mighty, in fact, it broke his jaw.